TOPIC BOOKS

Space

Fiona Macdonald

W
FRANKLIN WATTS
A Division of Grolier Publishing
NEW YORK • LONDON • HONG KONG • SYDNEY
DANBURY, CONNECTICUT

Cover: Bruce Coleman (main image); Still Pictures /
Mike Phillips (inset).

Interior Pictures:
Illustrations: Peter Bull 5, 7, 8, 10, 11, 14l, 18, 21; Sarah
John 9, 12, 23; Carolyn Scrace 14r, 15, 17, 26.
Photography: European Space Organisation 4 (inset);
NASA 20b; NASA/Science Photo Library 24, 25 (all);
Photodisc copyright page, 4 (main), 6, 8, 10, 11, 12, 18, 19
(both), 20t, 21, 22, 23, 27, 28, 29; Science Photo Library
16t (David Parker), 16b Stephen & Donna O'Meara).

Acknowledgement: Page 13 'Moon Poem' by Vachel Lindsay from
Congo and Other Poems, originally published by Macmillan Co.,
New York, 1915 and now available on the American Verse Project
‹http://wwwhti.umich.edu/english/amverse/› is reproduced with
permission of The University of Michigan Press.

Series editor: Helen Lanz
Series designer: John Christopher, WHITE DESIGN
Picture research: Sue Mennell
Illustrators: Peter Bull, Sarah John and Carolyn Scrace
Consultant: Dot Jackson
Space consultant: Stuart Clark

First published in 1999 by
Franklin Watts
96 Leonard Street
London
EC2A 4XD

First American edition 2000 by Franklin Watts
A Division of Grolier Publishing
90 Sherman Turnpike
Danbury, CT 06816

Visit Franklin Watts on the Internet at
http://publishing.grolier.com

Catalog details are available from the Library of Congress
Cataloging-in-Publication Data.

ISBN 0-531-14542-5 (lib.bdg.) 0-531-15426-2

Copyright © Franklin Watts 1999
Printed in Hong Kong/China

Contents

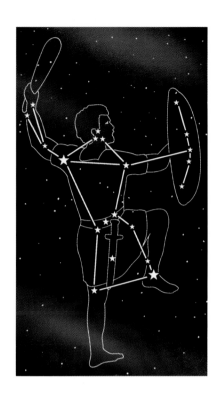

The Universe

Space is what we see when we look into the night sky. It is everything that exists beyond Earth's atmosphere.

Earth in Space

The atmosphere is a layer of air about 620 miles (1,000 km) thick surrounding Earth. It is made up of invisible gases, such as oxygen and carbon dioxide, that are needed for life on Earth.

There is no barrier between the end of Earth's atmosphere and the beginning of space: The two blend into one another. Earth is in space; it is in its own galaxy. A galaxy is a group of stars.

Space Words

Many different words are used to describe space. See if you can find these words as you look through this book and discover what they mean:

star	astronomer
sun	gravity
Moon	interstellar matter
planet	
universe	neutron star
galaxy	nebula
protostar	solar system
supernova	orbit
constellation	

▶ This is NGC 1323, a spiral-shaped galaxy. A galaxy is made up of billions of stars. There is no air in space, but there are clouds of gas and space dust within each galaxy.

The Beginning of the Universe

We do not know exactly when the universe began. A few scientists believe that the universe has always been there, with no beginning and no end. But most scientists think that the universe began about 14 billion years ago. They think it started from a tiny point and exploded into life in a "Big Bang." After the Big Bang, the universe expanded very, very fast. Stars, planets, and everything else in space was created. The universe is still expanding today.

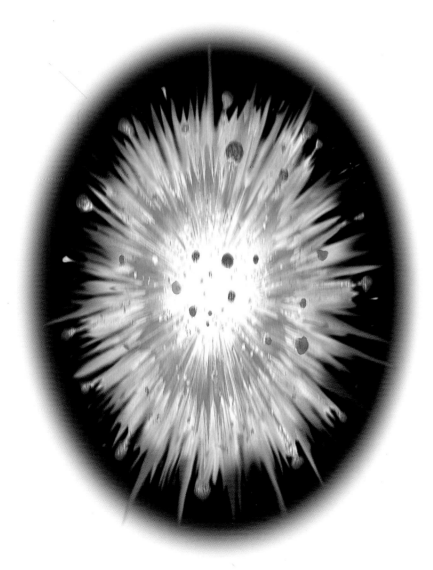

Did You Know...

"Universe" is our word for space and all that it contains: stars, galaxies, suns, moons, planets, comets, and meteors. You can find out more about all these in this book.

There can be hundreds of billions of stars in a galaxy, and there are billions of galaxies in the universe.

The distances within space are so vast that scientists use a unit of length called a light-year to measure them.

A light-year is the distance that light travels in one year. It is about 6 billion miles (10 billion km).

Distances in Space

Nobody knows how big space is. Measuring space is a puzzle that scientists still face today. Some scientists think that space has no center and no boundaries: It goes on forever.

The Sun in Our Solar System

The sun we see is one of many billions of stars in the universe. Like all stars, it is a huge ball of glowing gases. Scientists think that the sun was formed about 4.5 billion years ago, when a cloud of gas in space began to shrink. As it got smaller, it got hotter. Today, the surface temperature of the sun is 11,000°F (6,000°C), and its inside is 27,000,000°F (15,000,000°C).

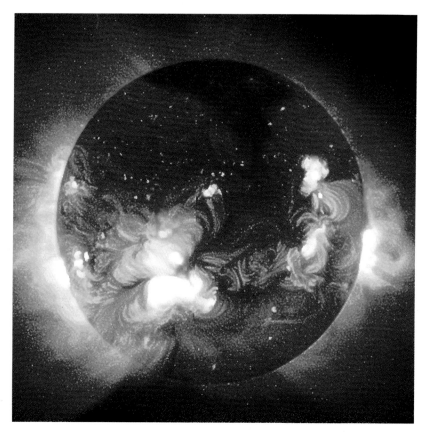

◀ *Because the sun is so hot, it gives out rays of heat and light. We can feel them and see them here on Earth. Without the heat and light from the sun, life on Earth would not exist.*

Our Solar System

The sun is surrounded by nine planets, which orbit, or travel around, the sun all the time. They are pulled toward the Sun, and held in their orbits, by an invisible force called gravity (*see right*). If there were no gravity, the planets would float away into space. Together, the sun and its nine planets are called the solar system. Solar means "belonging to the sun."

➥ *The nine planets in our solar system are Mercury, Venus, Earth, Mars, Jupiter, Saturn, Uranus, Neptune, and Pluto.*

Did You Know...

Gravity is an invisible force between things; it pulls things together. There is a pull of gravity between all objects, big and small. The bigger the mass of an object, the stronger the pull of its gravity. (Mass means how much matter, or stuff, there is in an object). Objects with a lot of mass pull objects with less mass toward them.

Mercury, Venus, Earth, and Mars are made from rock. Mercury is the closest planet to the sun.

Jupiter, Saturn, and Uranus are made mostly from gases and liquids.

Pluto, the outermost planet, is made of ice and rock.

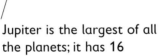

Jupiter is the largest of all the planets; it has **16** moons of its own.

YOU CAN TRY THIS!

Try This! The Pull of Gravity

Gravity is the force that makes things fall to the ground when we drop them. Earth has more mass than anything on it, so it has stronger gravity and pulls things toward its center. Earth's gravity pulls all objects toward it with the same amount of force, whether they are light or heavy.

To test this, find two objects of about the same size and shape, but of different weights — a heavy football and a lightweight beach ball. Drop them — carefully! — from a window. They should reach the ground at the same time.

Earth in Space

Although we cannot feel it, Earth is traveling through space all the time.

Day and Night

As Earth travels through space, it spins around and around an imaginary line called its axis. It takes 24 hours to complete each spin. The side of Earth facing the sun has light in daytime: the side facing away from the sun has dark in nightime.

◀ *This picture of Earth, taken from space, shows both day and night on Earth.*

The Earth's Orbit

As Earth spins on its axis, it also travels around the sun. It takes the Earth 365$\frac{1}{4}$ days (a whole year) to orbit the sun. Earth's axis is tilted: This means that different parts of Earth get closer to the sun as Earth travels around it. This makes the seasons change in many countries from warm summer to cold winter.

The Earth spins counterclockwise around the sun. As it moves, different countries face toward the sun.

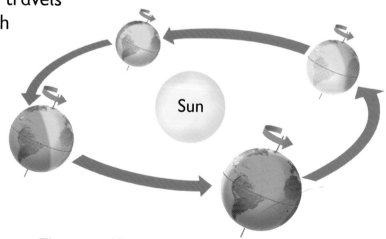

The parts of Earth tilted toward the sun have summer, the parts tilted away from the sun have winter.

HOW THE EARTH WAS MADE

Ever since people first lived on Earth, they have made up stories to explain how the Earth was made. Almost every civilization had creation myths of its own. This story comes from ancient Egypt.

In the beginning, there was nothing. Nothing at all. No sun and moon; no Earth and sky. No wind or water. Just nothing.

Then, magically, using all his wisdom, the Sun God created himself. He named himself Atun, which means "everything" or "completeness." It was a good name: he was all there was. All the future depended on him.

Atun, the Sun God, shone brightly. He felt full of energy. But there was no air for him to warm, or water to reflect his rays. So he sneezed — and the misty Air God, Shu, hovered and shimmered close by. Atun was pleased. He spat and the Water Goddess, Tefnut, glittered into life at his feet. Now there was warmth, light, air, and moisture — everything needed to support living things.

Shu was handsome and Tefnut was beautiful. They married; their children were Nut (the starry Sky) and Geb (strong, solid Earth). Together, Geb and Nut, the Earth and Sky, created many lesser gods and goddesses — and all the ordinary men and women who live on planet Earth.

Every time the Egyptians looked up and saw Atun rise, climb high in the sky, then sink down again at sunset, they said "Look! Atun is still at work. Every day, he gives new life and energy to our world."

How the Earth Was Made

Scientists believe our solar system was made from a spinning cloud of gas and dust that orbited the center of our galaxy. About 6 billion years ago, this cloud collapsed into a disc shape. The sun formed at its center. Dust particles in the spinning cloud collided and stuck together in clumps.

After about 100 million years, the particles had grown so large that they became the planets in our solar system, including Earth. At first, the young planets were so hot, they were molten (melted). They cooled, and some became solid. This happened to Earth about 4.5 billion years ago.

Stars and Galaxies

Like our sun, the stars that we see in the night sky are balls of hot gas. They measure thousands or millions of miles across, but look tiny because they are so far away. All stars give off light. Although all stars move, many of them appear fixed in the same position in the sky.

Some stars are grouped together in galaxies. Our solar system is part of a vast, spiral-shaped galaxy called the Milky Way. (It was given this name because it looks like a trickle of milky light flowing across the night sky.)

➤ *This is the Milky Way. The very bright patch of light in the center is Hale-Bopp comet.*

Did You Know...

Neutron stars are very small stars. Neutron stars that spin around are called pulsars. Some neutron stars become so small that no light — or anything else — can escape from them. They are then known as black holes.

The Life Cycle of Stars

Stars change how they look, depending on how old or young they are.

Space dust and gas form clouds, called nebulae.

Balls of gas, called protostars, form inside nebulae.

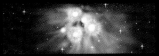

The protostars get amazingly hot, and explosions begin inside.

They are now main-sequence stars and live for over 10 million years.

As the stars use up some of their energy, they change size and become extremely bright (giants or supergiants). Supergiants are the brightest, hottest stars.

Old stars either explode (supernova) or fade away (white dwarf). Brown dwarves are failed stars.

Space Matter

When the sun and the planets formed, other pieces of rock and ice were left behind in space. They are called interstellar matter and include comets, asteroids, and shooting stars.

Comets are balls of ice and frozen gases mixed with grit and dust. They orbit the sun, but follow a different path from Earth's orbit.

Asteroids are made of rock. They also orbit the sun — mainly between Mars and Jupiter.

Shooting stars are not stars at all but streaks of bright light in the sky. They occur when pieces of space dust enter Earth's atmosphere and catch fire. Most shooting stars are tiny and burn up before they reach Earth's surface, but a few are big enough to survive the journey and crash into Earth.

◆ *The scientific name for shooting stars is "meteors." Pieces of a large meteor that crash to Earth are called meteorites. This huge crater has been made by a meteorite.*

The Moon

The moon is our neighbor in space. It is about 239,000 miles (384,400 km) away. Like Earth, the moon is made of rock, but it has no atmosphere and no water. The surface of the moon is covered with mountains, dry "seas", and enormous craters.

▶ *The moon does not give out any light of its own. It shines because it reflects some of the light that falls on it from the sun.*

New Moon

Crescent

Half

Crescent

Half

Waxing

Waning

Full Moon

The moon orbits Earth, as Earth orbits the sun. The moon takes $27\frac{1}{3}$ days to travel around Earth. It travels at just over 6/10 mile (1 km) per second. As it travels through space the moon spins on its axis, like Earth (*see page 8*). But because of the time it takes to spin, it always keeps the same side facing Earth. No one knew what the far side of the moon looked like until 1959, when it was photographed by a Russian spacecraft.

◀ *During the moon's orbit of Earth, it seems to change shape. This is because people on Earth can see different parts of the moon lit up by the sun.*

Did You Know...

Many other planets have moons that travel around them. There are at least 60 moons in the solar system all together. Venus and Mercury are the only planets without moons. Earth and Pluto have one each. Saturn is the planet with the most moons. It has 20 known moons, plus probably many others — so far undiscovered — hidden in its rings. The moons are held in orbit around the planets by gravity, just as gravity holds the planets in orbit around the sun.

MOON POEM

The Moon's the North Wind's cookie.
He bites it day by day,
Until there's but a rim of scraps
That crumble all away.

The South Wind is a baker.
He kneads clouds in his den.
And bakes a crisp new moon that... greedy
North... Wind... eats... again!

VACHEL LINDSAY

Try This! Moon Cookies

You will need: 6 tablespoons melted butter • 1/2 cup sugar • 2 tablespoons corn syrup • 1 cup oatmeal • 1/2 cup flour • 1 egg

1 Measure all the ingredients shown. Turn the oven on to 350°F (180°C).

2 Put the butter into a saucepan. Ask an adult to turn stove to medium heat. Melt the butter in the saucepan and leave to cool.

3 Mix the sugar, flour, and oatmeal in a bowl.

4 Beat the egg in a cup.

5 Pour the egg, melted butter, and corn syrup into the sugar, flour, and oatmeal. Mix well.

6 Now the mixture should be dough-like. Shape it into walnut-sized balls.

7 Grease a baking sheet with a thin layer of butter. Place the balls of mixture onto the tray about 3/4 in (2 cm) apart. Flatten slightly.

8 Put the cookies into the heated oven for about 15 minutes.

9 When the cookies are golden, ask an adult to take the baking sheet from the oven. Let the cookies cool, then lift them off the sheet.

Constellations

Constellations are groups of stars in the night sky: People imagine that they make pictures. In the past, people gave these star-pictures names. They named them after gods, animals, and important objects. Constellation names include Leo (the Lion), Ursa Major (the Great Bear) and Orion (a Mighty Hunter).

Most of the stars in each constellation are not linked together — they may be hundreds of light-years apart. The stars just happen to make a picture when viewed from Earth. Today there are 88 constellations recognized by astronomers — scientists who study the stars.

◀ This shows the constellation of Orion, and the outline that people were reminded of — the mighty hunter himself.

Astronomers use the names of constellations to map different parts of the sky. For example, a star might be described as "the southernmost star in Orion."

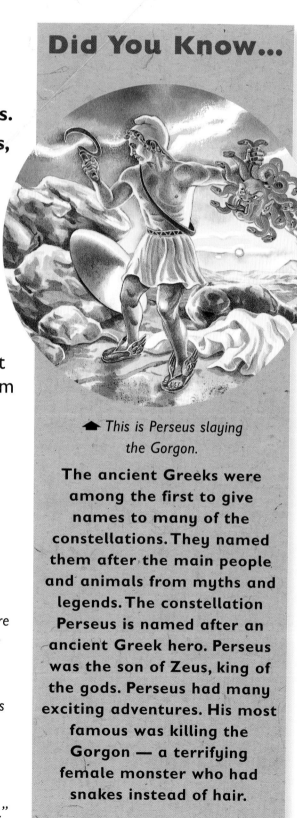

Did You Know...

◀ This is Perseus slaying the Gorgon.

The ancient Greeks were among the first to give names to many of the constellations. They named them after the main people and animals from myths and legends. The constellation Perseus is named after an ancient Greek hero. Perseus was the son of Zeus, king of the gods. Perseus had many exciting adventures. His most famous was killing the Gorgon — a terrifying female monster who had snakes instead of hair.

Try This! Can You See the Mighty Hunter?

Orion is a constellation inside a nebula (a cloud of gas and dust, *see page 11*). It is about 1,500 light-years away. You can see Orion in wintertime in the Northern Hemisphere and six months later, in wintertime in the Southern Hemisphere.

You will need:
• a compass
• a flashlight
• a star map from an astronomy book
• warm clothing

Get a trusted adult to accompany you for this observation. Do not go out at night without permission. Never go out to look at the stars alone.

ASK AN ADULT

1 Find a dark spot, away from too much light from street lamps, shops, or houses.

2 Using the compass and a star map, can you find Orion in the sky?

3 Look for the four bright stars that make up Orion's body. Betelgeuse, one of the brightest stars in the sky, is at his right shoulder. Bellatrix is his left shoulder. Saiph and Rigel highlight his two legs. Three brilliant stars, in line, form Orion's belt.

YOU CAN TRY THIS!

Investigating Space

For thousands of years, people have tried to find out more about space. They have used many different methods.

▶ *Stonehenge may be an early observatory — a place where people look at the moon and stars. It dates back to 2100 B.C. The position of the stones line up with the movements of the sun. People believe that Stonehenge was used for festivals at sunrise.*

➤ *The Mauna Kea observatory in Hawaii has a vast optical telescope. It is 13,800 ft (4,200 m) above sea level, on the top of a dormant (sleeping) volcano. The air is so clear that it makes Mauna Kea one of the best observatories in the world.*

Space Information

Special types of jet planes, sounding rockets, and balloons have all been used to carry equipment into space. The equipment records information that is sent back to Earth. Modern ways to collect information about space include photometry. This is a special way of measuring the light from stars, and other objects in space, that travels to Earth.

Optical telescopes make objects that are far away appear larger. They were used in the days of Galileo Galilei (see box). Huge modern optical telescopes are now used, such as the one at Mauna Kea (bottom left).

Galileo Galilei

Italian scientist Galileo Galilei lived from 1564-1642. At that time, people believed that Earth was the center of the universe. They also believed that the sun traveled around Earth.

Galileo was a brilliant mathematician. He was also one of the first people to look at the moon and stars through a telescope, which had only just been invented. Many years earlier, another scientist, Copernicus, believed that Earth was not the center of the universe, and that Earth traveled around the sun. By using his mathematical skills, and from what he saw through the telescope, Galileo began to think that Copernicus had been right.

Today, we know that both these claims are true, but in Galileo's time they were shocking. They upset powerful leaders of the Christian Church who thought that Galileo was criticizing their traditional teachings about how God made the universe. Galileo was forced to apologize publicly to the Church. But he always believed his discoveries were true.

Is Anybody Out There?

The universe is so vast that many people believe there must be another planet, like Earth, that has the elements needed for life: light, heat, water, and the gases oxygen and carbon dioxide.

▶ *During the past 50 years, scientists have carried out experiments to see whether they can pick up any radio messages or electrical signals sent from distant planets that show there is life somewhere else. They have not been successful so far.*

◀ *Scientists have also designed a "message in pictures" and fitted it to long-distance space probes (see page 20). It is designed to tell anyone who sees it what Earth and human beings are like — even if they don't know how to use words.*

Try This! A Message to Space

Imagine that you are a mission commander on board a spaceship. You are planning a long voyage to a distant planet. You hope to meet space creatures on your journey, and you want to show them what life on Earth is like. So you pack a box with ten carefully chosen objects, and write them a letter telling them who you are and why you are traveling. (You know that they probably won't read or write like you do, so you write as much of your letter as you can in pictures.)

Which ten objects would you include? Make a drawing to show them. Add labels to say what they are and why you have chosen them.

Write a picture-letter explaining who you are and why you are traveling through space.

YOU CAN TRY THIS!

Satellites and Probes

A satellite is an object that orbits a planet or star. The world's first artificial satellite, Sputnik, was launched in 1957. ("Sputnik" is a Russian word meaning "traveling companion.") Since then, many thousands of satellites have been sent into space.

▲ This picture of Earth is taken from a satellite. Photos like this are used to help forecast weather. They can also help search for valuable minerals, such as oil, below Earth's surface.

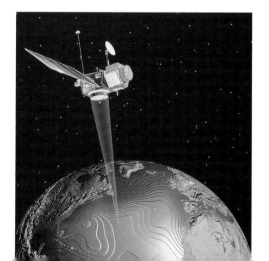

Information from satellites (left) is sent back to people on Earth and used for many purposes. Some artificial satellites are used to investigate space. Others help ships navigate (find their way) at sea. Satellites have changed the way we communicate. They are used for making long-distance phone calls and to send radio and television programs around the world. The Internet would be impossible without them.

▶ *This space probe, Galileo, was sent into space in 1995 to gather information about Jupiter.*

Space Probes

Probes are spacecraft that carry instruments but no people. They are designed to explore parts of the solar system that are too far away, or too dangerous, for people to visit.

Probes carry equipment that collects and records information about space. Their cameras can take close-up pictures 20 or 30 times more detailed than anything that can be taken from Earth. Their long antennae can pick up faint radio waves coming from stars, and their delicate sensors can detect invisible cosmic rays. Transmitters send this information back to Earth.

▼ *This image shows the surface of Mars. It was taken by a small wheeled robot, Sojourner, that was put on Mars by the space probe Viking Pathfinder.*

Did You Know...

So many objects have been launched into space that some scientists think it will soon become too crowded up there. As well as satellites and spacecraft, many tons of "space junk" are also orbiting, such as failed or worn-out satellites and bits of broken spacecraft. Scientists fear a dangerous collision between the space junk and a valuable satellite, or a spacecraft with astronauts on board.

The Space Age

We live in the space age. Since the 1920s, rockets, animals, men, and women have traveled away from Earth to fly in space.

The Space Race

During the 1950s and 1960s, America and the Soviet Union, then the two most powerful nations in the world, competed with each other in the "space race." Each country's government believed that they could show the rest of the world how great their nations were by being the best at space technology. The space race lasted from 1957 to 1969.

◀ *"That's one small step for a man, one giant leap for mankind."* With these words, the first astronaut stepped onto the moon.

Timeline: Space Firsts

1926	First launch of a liquid-fueled rocket (USA).
1957	Satellite Sputnik I (USSR) makes the first-ever orbit around Earth.
1957	Satellite Sputnik 2 (USSR) carries the first-ever animal into space.
1951	Probe Luna 1 (USSR) is the first spacecraft to break free of Earth's gravity.
1961	Yuri Gagarin (USSR) is the first man in space.
1963	Valentina Tereshkova (USSR) is the first woman in space.
1965	First spacewalk, by Alexei Leonov (USSR).
1969	Apollo II (USA) lands first man (Neil Armstrong) on the moon.
1971	First manned space station, Salyut (USSR).
1976	Viking I (USA) makes the first landing on Mars.
1981	First flight of the space shuttle (USA).

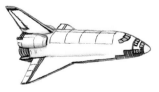

1986	First permanently inhabited space station, Mir (USSR).
1990	Hubble Space Telescope (USA) is launched.

Rockets

Rockets are the most powerful engines ever made. They are the only kind of engine that can create a strong enough force (called thrust) to break away from Earth's gravity (look back to page 7), and push their way into space.

▶ *Here, the space shuttle is launched from Cape Canaveral, Florida. The space shuttle is the only spacecraft that lands back on Earth.*

Rocket Power

A rocket is powered by jets (powerful blasts) of hot gases shooting out of a nozzle at the back. The jets push the rocket forward. The blasts are caused by a reaction in the engine between the fuel and explosive gases, called oxidizers.

To make them burn, all fuels need a gas called oxygen. There is plenty of oxygen in Earth's atmosphere, but no oxygen in space. Rockets always carry sources of oxygen to make sure they can be powered at all times.

Did You Know...

The first rockets were invented in China. In 1232, armies from Mongolia attacked the walled city of Kiafeng. The citizens fought back by throwing home-made rockets at the attackers. These were tubes filled with explosive powder attached to long bamboo poles. The Chinese called their rockets "arrows of flying fire."

Space Shuttle

The U.S. space shuttle is powered by two different kinds of rocket. Booster rockets, using solid fuel, push the shuttle away from Earth's gravity. Each one produces 2.6 million pounds (1.2 million kilograms) of thrust. A rocket powered by a tank of liquid hydrogen gas is used to push the shuttle into space.

Try This! Rocket Balloon

You can see how rockets work by blowing up a balloon, then letting it go. A jet of gases (the breath you have puffed inside) streams out of the balloon's nozzle, pushing it forward through the air. The more breath you force inside the balloon, the greater "rocket power" it will have.

FLORIDA NEWS

DATELINE OCTOBER 29, 1998

Risky business
From our Florida reporter

Today, veteran astronaut John Glenn (77) returned to space, 36 years after his earlier record-breaking flight. On February 20, 1962, he became the first American to orbit Earth, proving that it was possible to fly right around the world.

Glenn's first spaceflight was made alone, crammed into a tiny space capsule, with only rockets and parachutes to help it land.

Space travel has changed dramatically since then. Today, U.S. astronauts travel on board the re-usable space shuttle, which has room for seven and glides gracefully back to Earth.

sitting on top of a bomb

But space travel is still a risky business. Each spacecraft is still blasted away from Earth by massive rockets which can sometimes disastrously explode. One astronaut has described the launch process as like sitting on top of a bomb.

Since Glenn's first spaceflight there have been several tragic accidents in space. In January 1986, space shuttle Challenger exploded 73 seconds after takeoff. All seven crew members were killed. Scientists have worked to reduce the risks of space travel. Even so, many risks remain.

undaunted as he boarded the spacecraft

But Glenn seemed undaunted as he boarded the spacecraft, waved on by well-wishers who had come to honor an American hero on his second adventure into space.

Life Support in Space

Space is a hostile environment. People, animals, and plants that have evolved, or developed, to live on Earth cannot survive in space without help. They need special life-support systems to provide them with air, food, and water. They also need to be protected from extreme heat and cold, and dangerous cosmic rays.

If astronauts plan to spend more than a few hours in space, their life-support system also has to get rid of body waste. They need somewhere to sleep, exercise, wash, and brush their teeth. All these facilities have to work in zero, or very low, gravity (see page 7). In space there is no gravity, so everything is weightless and will float around unless it is strapped down.

◄ *Preparing space food. There are four types of food: dried, pre-cooked and partially dried, chilled, and frozen. Food is stored in plastic envelopes or aluminum cans. Drinks come as powders — astronauts mix them with hot or cold water. Astronauts have to drink more in space than on Earth.*

Waste management. This spacecraft toilet has grips that the astronauts put over their thighs and feet to keep them on the seat, but otherwise it is similar to toilets on Earth. Solid and liquid waste is collected by air-jets, and solid waste is crushed and sealed in plastic bags. All solid waste and trash is stored and returned to Earth.

This shower is being developed for use in space. A vacuum sucks out extra water. Because of zero gravity, there is a foot and hand grip.

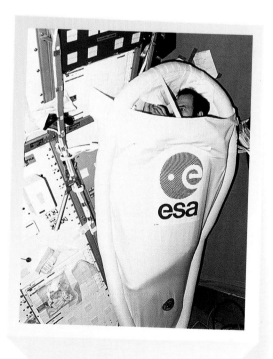

There are no beds in space. Astronauts sleep in sleeping bags, hung from the spacecraft ceiling. Because of zero gravity, there is no feeling of lying down. Astronauts say that weightlessness affects their dreams.

Did You Know...

Astronauts who return to Earth after a long flight sometimes cannot walk, or even stand up, for a while. Their muscles have wasted away in space. They need a careful exercise program to build them up again.

Space Settlement

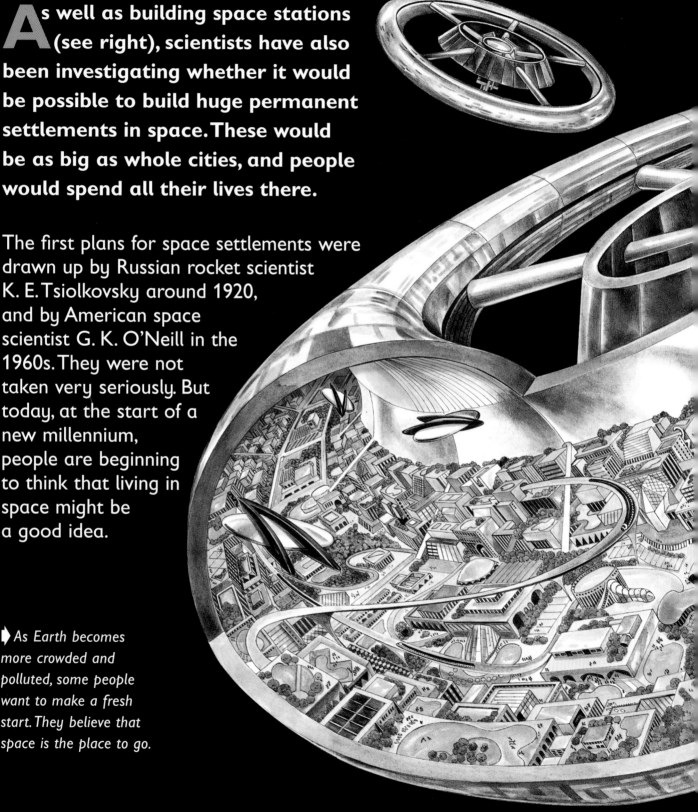

As well as building space stations (see right), scientists have also been investigating whether it would be possible to build huge permanent settlements in space. These would be as big as whole cities, and people would spend all their lives there.

The first plans for space settlements were drawn up by Russian rocket scientist K. E. Tsiolkovsky around 1920, and by American space scientist G. K. O'Neill in the 1960s. They were not taken very seriously. But today, at the start of a new millennium, people are beginning to think that living in space might be a good idea.

▶ As Earth becomes more crowded and polluted, some people want to make a fresh start. They believe that space is the place to go.

Space Stations

Space stations are permanent or semi-permanent bases in space. Astronauts live on board for months at a time to make observations and carry out scientific experiments. The first space station, Salyut, was launched by the Soviet Union in 1971. In 1986, the Soviet Union launched a new, more advanced space station called Mir (Peace). Today, a huge new international space station is being built. It will be launched from the United States.

Space experiments include looking at the effect on the body of space travel and of being weightless for long periods of time.

◀ *By 1999, the Mir space station had become too expensive to keep in space and was allowed to break up.*

Try This! Low-Gravity Games

Space settlements would be designed to have artificial gravity to make life inside them almost like life on Earth. However, there might be one special place in each space settlement left with low gravity for people to use for sports and games.

Because of this low gravity, people can jump at least six times higher in space than on Earth.

1 Measure how far you can step in a single stride.

2 Then measure how far you can jump from standing.

3 Measure how high you can jump.

4 Write down all your results.

Now imagine you are visiting several different space settlements. They each have low-gravity sports areas.

5 How far could you step if low gravity let you step 4 times, 11 times, and 13 times farther than on Earth?

6 How far could you jump from standing if low gravity let you jump 5 times, 12 times, and 14 times farther than on Earth?

7 How high could you jump if low gravity let you jump 2, 8 and 19 times higher than on Earth?

What's More...

Is the Universe Changing?

Old stars are fading away and new stars are being made all the time. Most scientists also think that the universe is still expanding.

Will the Universe Come to an End?

Scientists don't know if the universe will end. It depends on whether it goes on expanding, or whether it shrinks. If the universe continues to expand, all the energy in the stars will be used up. The universe will become completely dark, but it will go on expanding forever. If the universe begins to shrink, then it could end just as it began. It would collapse into a tiny single point in a second Big Bang. From there it could possibly be re-created all over again. But that won't be for several billion years yet!

◀ *This photograph shows many galaxies. It was sent back to Earth by the giant Hubble Space Telescope.*

UFOs

As well as looking for life in space, some people hope that aliens (creatures from other worlds) might come to Earth.

About 100 years ago, people reported seeing balloon-like "mystery ships" in the skies over the United States. These were the first reports of UFOs — Unidentified Flying Objects — and people thought they came from space. Since then, thousands of sightings have been reported, including metal "foo fighters," which hovered around fighter planes in World War II (1939–1945), and the first "flying saucers," spotted by an American pilot over Washington in 1947.

Nearly all UFOs can be explained scientifically. Many are unusual effects produced by natural forces, such as rain, clouds, and sunlight. Some are due to people having hallucinations (waking dreams). Some are tricks. But a few have never been properly explained and the mystery remains...

▲ *Natural phenomena such as the Southern Lights, which look like stars dancing in the sky, have led people to believe they have seen a UFO.*

YOU CAN TRY THIS!

Try This! Constellation Picture

You will need: black or dark blue paper • stick-on stars • gold or silver paint and brushes or gold and silver pens • scrap paper

1 *Choose a constellation you would like to draw (see page 14). Plan a design for your picture on a piece of scrap paper.*

2 *Mark where you want to stick the stars, and where you will draw lines.*

3 *Then copy your design onto the black or dark blue paper.*

4 *Stick on the stars and finish off your picture by drawing in the shape of your chosen constellation in silver or gold.*

Glossary

antennae: Sensitive aerials that pick up faint radio waves.

asteroid: Small, rocky objects in the solar system. They are made when larger objects break up. Some may be the remains of comets.

astronomer: A scientist who studies space.

atmosphere: layer of air about 620 miles (1,000 km) thick surrounding Earth.

axis: An invisible line running through the middle of Earth from the North Pole to the South Pole.

billion: One thousand million (1,000,000,000).

brown dwarf: A failed star that is too small to shine.

comet: Balls of ice and frozen gases mixed with grit and dust. They orbit the sun.

constellation: Groups of stars that people link together in their mind's eye to make pictures in the sky.

cosmic rays: High-speed, invisible rays sent out by the sun and other stars. They harm all living creatures. Astronauts have to wear special clothing to protect them from cosmic rays.

galaxy: A group of stars.

gravity: An invisible force between objects; it pulls things together. The bigger the mass of an object, the stronger the pull of its gravity.

light-year: The distance that light travels in one year; about 6 billion miles (10 billion km).

main-sequence stars: Stars in the longest, steadiest part of their life cycle.

mass: The amount of matter (stuff) there is in an object.

meteor: The scientific name for "shooting star" (see page 31).

meteorite: A large meteor that falls to Earth.

nebula (plural: nebulae): Cloud of space dust and gas.

neutron star: A very small star that collapses.

nova: A star that suddenly increases in brightness, then quickly fades away.

Glossary

observatory: A place where astronomers study space and the stars.

optical telescope: A telescope that uses lenses and mirrors to allow us to see things that are far away.

orbit: The path of a satellite, moon or planet as it travels around the Earth or another large object in space.

photometry: A special way of measuring the light from stars and other objects in space that travels to Earth.

planets: Nine very large "bodies" (some made of rock, some made of gas) that orbit the sun. Their names are Mercury, Venus, Earth, Mars, Jupiter, Saturn, Uranus, Neptune, and Pluto.

probes: Spacecraft that explore distant parts of the solar system. They carry scientific instruments but no people.

protostars: Balls of hot gas that form inside nebulae.

pulsar: Neutron star that spins around and around.

satellite: An object that travels round a planet or a star.

shooting star: Streaks of bright light in the sky. They occur when pieces of space dust enter the Earth's atmosphere and catch fire.

solar system: The sun and all the objects that orbit it.

sounding rocket: Rocket carrying scientific instruments.

space dust: Tiny fragments of rock in space, created when asteroids and meteors collide with other objects in space. Some space dust is also scattered by comets.

space station: A permanent or semi-permanent base in space where astronauts go to study space.

star: A ball of hot, glowing gas.

supergiants: The hottest, brightest stars.

supernova: An old star that has exploded.

universe: Space and all that it contains, such as stars, galaxies, suns, moons, planets, comets, and meteors.

Index